**I CAN**

PLAY
FOOTBALL

SHEILA FRASER
AND
LISA KOPPER

Franklin Watts
London · New York · Toronto · Sydney

My name's Shaun. I want to play football.
One day I'm going to be really good.
Dad says it's best to play in the park.
There's a special place for practising
ball games. We go there a lot.

It's fun running and kicking.
Sometimes I miss altogether.
Sometimes I kick the ball hard
with my foot. Now I've hurt my toe.

"Try to use the side of your foot — your instep," says Dad.
"And keep watching the ball."

I have a go but it's not very easy.
Dad says to keep trying.

He puts two jumpers on the
ground and tells me to kick
the ball between them.

Usually I miss.

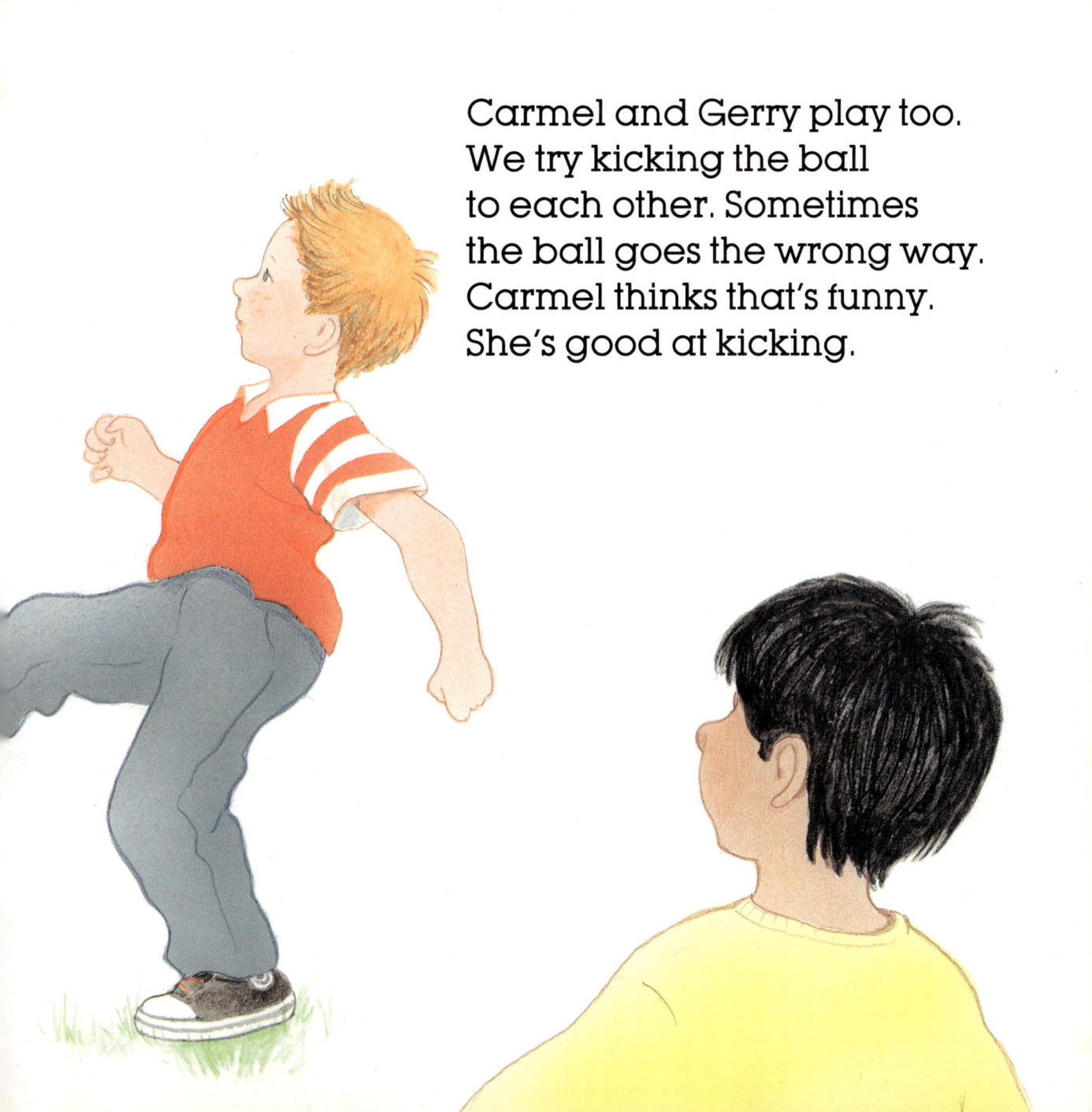

Carmel and Gerry play too.
We try kicking the ball
to each other. Sometimes
the ball goes the wrong way.
Carmel thinks that's funny.
She's good at kicking.

I try heading with Dad. We stand close together.
I think it might hurt my head if he throws too hard.
But he says "Use your forehead, not the top
of your head. Then you won't get a headache."

I did last time.

Next we try kicking balls into a bucket.
Carmel and Gerry can get theirs in the bucket
most of the time. I got mine in once.

Carmel and Gerry are good at juggling the ball too.
They can keep it off the ground for ages.
I drop it quite a lot. Why does it look so easy
when famous footballers do it?

We try to hit the numbers
on the wall. We start
with 1 and try to get to 8.
Even little Jodi thinks
she can do it. I kick the ball
too high. Carmel laughs.

Victoria can see that I feel silly.
It's not fair. Everyone else can do it.
Why can't I?

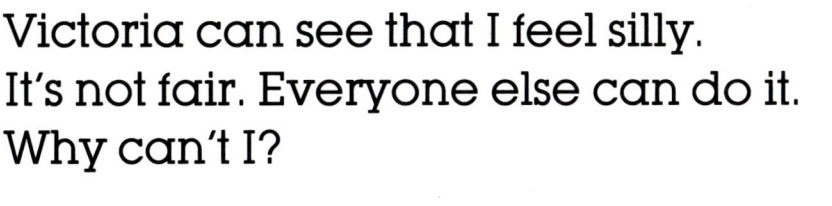

"Come on, Shaun. Cheer up,"
says Dad.
"There's going to be a game.
Nicholas will be goalkeeper."

There are 11 players in World Cup teams.
They have to learn lots of rules and practise
every day. We haven't got enough people
for a World Cup team. Victoria wants to be
in my team. There are only five of us.

We start to play. Gerry kicks the ball
to Carmel. Carmel kicks it to me.
And I kick it between the two jumpers.

"Hurray!" screams Carmel. "You scored a goal."
Gerry gives me a hug like real footballers do.

We start to play again and all the time
I think "I can do it. I didn't think I could,
but I can. I can play football."

What happened to Shaun?

Why is Carmel laughing?

How does Gerry practise?